C000195791

IN
FULL CRY

CONTENTS

IN FULL CRY
Jim Meads

Quiller Press

DEDICATION

I dedicate this book to all those generous foxhunters in North America, together with the American M.F.H.A., who, over the past twenty-eight years, have sponsored my visits to their hunts and shows, where the welcome has always been overwhelming. This includes the innumerable people who purchased copies of the pictures which I took while visiting. This was especially relevant during the foot and mouth crisis, when my work in the U.K. completely dried up. Thank you one and all.

The Publisher wishes to thank Clare Sawers and Jane Trowbridge for their assistance in the publication of this book.

Page 1 photograph: Barry Todhunter with Blencathra Hounds
Page 3 photograph: Taf Fechan Hunt

Baroness Mallalieu, who does so much to help hunting, not only in the House of Lords, but also in the countryside, regularly hunts with the Bicester with Whaddon Chase hounds. Here she is pictured, surrounded by hunt staff, at the Peterborough Royal Foxhound Show in 1999, when she was Show President.

Copyright © 2003 Jim Meads

First published in the UK in 2003
by Quiller Press, an imprint of Quiller Publishing Ltd

British Library Cataloguing-in-Publication Data
A catalogue record for this book
is available from the British Library

ISBN 1 904057 26 8

The information in this book is true and complete to the best of our knowledge. All recommendations are made without any guarantee on the part of the Publisher, who also disclaims any liability incurred in connection with the use of this data or specific details.

All rights reserved. No part of this book may be reproduced or transmitted in any form or by any means, electronic or mechanical including photocopying, recording or by any information storage and retrieval system, without permission from the Publisher in writing.

Printed in China

Quiller Press
an imprint of Quiller Publishing Ltd.
Wykey House, Wykey, Shrewsbury, SY4 1JA, England
Tel: 01939 261616 Fax: 01939 261606
E-mail: info@quillerbooks.com
Website: www.swanhillbooks.com

The first ever Lady President of The American MFHA, Daphne Flowers Wood MFH, riding her favourite hunter 'Derby' along a dirt road in Florida, during a hunt with her Live Oak Hounds.

FOREWORDS

I have heard it said that for those who do not understand the magic of hunting no explanation is possible and for those who do, no explanation is necessary. Perhaps that is true. How do you explain magic? How do you describe a passion, particularly to those who refuse to listen for fear that cherished preconceptions and prejudices may be destroyed by reason, or evidence or first-hand experience?

Many, like me, try to do it with words. The magic for us is sometimes to be found in the sheer overpowering beauty of a single image – dappled sunlight on dappled hounds racing through woodland, or when standing on the hill at first light and hearing the cautious note of a single hound in the mist joined by more and more until the whole valley explodes in a frenzy of music.

It is there too, at the end of the day in the laughter and comradeship of a troop of tired, happy, mud spattered hunters riding back in the failing light, horses' hooves striking sparks from the road as they pass.

Then there is the magic of the huntsman, controlling his straining pack as if each hound were held fast by an invisible lead until he releases them on the line of the stag with a single movement of his hand.

It is there again, in the eyes and ears and impatience of the old horse that listens and watches and notices hounds slip away, whilst his rider jokes with his friends – and does not.

Hunting is a deadly and seductive combination; unable-to-eat-breakfast anticipation, the heart thumping exhilaration of the fast gallop, the fears and the fences and a blissful physical tiredness like no other which follows the hot bath at the end of a perfect day. It is all these things and a thousand others. It is beauty, it is excitement, it is unpredictability and physical danger, friendship and community, people and animals. Each hunting day is an unscripted drama, the set is landscape and success or failure is determined by forces beyond the control or understanding of man.

I have also heard it said that a picture paints a thousand words. Perhaps, where mere words cannot explain. Jim Meads' pictures may do so. Those who have felt the magic will find it in this book. I hope those who, as yet, have not, will find a key in these superb photographs which leads them also to the pleasure which so many all over the world have, for generations, shared.

Baroness Ann Mallalieu
President, The Countryside Alliance

What an honor for Jim, our friend of long standing, to ask me to write the foreword to this, his fourth book. The photographic history of no other sport has been so meticulously and lovingly chronicled by just one photographer. If there is one person that anyone who is anybody in foxhunting, on either side of the Atlantic, instantly recognizes, it has to be Jim Meads. With this printing, Jim has visited and photographed 465 different packs of hounds, 80 of which are in North America. What a fascinating career it has been, to be where the action is with so many varied packs of hounds. Like the late Capt. Wallace, Jim always turns up in the right spot with no apparent great hurry or effort. The result is literally thousands of spectacular photographs that showcase the varied places and faces that represent the vastness of our far flung sport.

These pages, like all of Jim's previous out of print collectable books, highlight the egalitarian nature and diversity of our passion. In the hunting field, the Duke and the dustman are on totally equal terms. This playing field, alone in all of sport, is level to all in that men, women, children, old, young, wealthy and poor are judged by only these criteria; their proficiency in the hunting field, their love of the sport, their knowledge of hounds and their total dedication to the future well being of their own hunts and foxhunting wherever it takes place. Their diverse ways of demonstrating ability and commitment run the gamut from tiny children flying enormous fences to invaluable old unmounted foxhunters standing on a hillside revelling in the sight of their beloved hounds drawing well despite hideous weather.

It is the diversity of fox hunting's participants that is its greatest strength. This was never demonstrated more aptly than at the Countryside Alliance march in London on 22nd September, 2002, when 408,000 plus people trekked to a huge city many of them had never been to before, and don't care to go to again, to defend their freedom and their right to hunt.

My husband Marty and I led the North American contingent, almost 100 strong to add our small 'Hell No' to the Labor Government's proposal to ban hunting. There we were, with hundreds of thousands of like minded people, many of whom are willing to go to jail for foxhunting, when their previous criminal records show not so much as a parking ticket!

As if by magic, out of the crowd popped Jim, camera in hand, to greet us and take a treasured picture of part of our group on Westminster Bridge waving an American flag and blowing a hunting horn.

Jim, you are a fabulous ambassador for our sport and long may you continue. They may not always 'meet at eleven', but you may rest assured that hounds WILL always meet all over the world at whatever time scent might be best! We shall see to that.

Daphne Flowers Wood MFH,
The first ever Lady President of The American MFHA.

INTRODUCTION

When I left the Royal Air Force in May 1950, after completing my two years National Service, as a lorry driver, not as a pilot or a photographer as I'd hoped, I began my career as a self-employed sporting photographer, little guessing what the future held for me. Now, writing this introduction to my fourth book, covering foxhunting and hare-hunting in the U.K. and North America, I find it difficult to comprehend two basic facts. Firstly, that in May 2003 I began my fifty-fourth consecutive season in this cut-throat profession, which I love, specialising in all aspect of our great sport, while always endeavouring to be in the right place at the right time, to capture the action or that spectacular setting. As I am completely self-taught and take pictures by instinct and experience, I will have to leave you, the reader, to decide whether or not I have succeeded.

Of course, cameras and films have improved out of all recognition since 1950, when I began work with what was already a 'vintage' Thornton Pickard Press Camera. This old 'bellows' camera took pictures on 5 x 4" glass plates, but had no exposure meter or range finder, so the distance to the subject and how much light was available, was pure guesswork. Amazingly, I still use this method to check that my present 'old faithful' cameras, Canon T-90s, are working correctly. Regarding films; the oldest colour photo in the book, taken in 1957, is the one on

page 108 of Sir Peter Farquhar MFH, with the Portman Hounds, posing on Okeford Hill in Dorset, on the way to a meet. For the technically minded, this was taken on a 5 x 4" sheet film, rated at 25 ASA, so unless it was a bright day and the subject stationary, it was a waste of time pressing the trigger. The second fact which I find difficult to comprehend, although I have photographic evidence to prove the figures, is that over the past fifty-three seasons, I have somehow managed to go out with and photograph no fewer than 465 different packs of hounds. This, I am led to believe, is a world record.

In the early days of my career, when the legend of 'The Running Photographer' was in its infancy, I often went out with three packs in one day. As an example, I quote from my hunting diary, an entry which is twenty-one years into my long varied and arduous working life. Saturday 18 September 1971: Leave home at 4am and drive 140 miles, to the 7.30 meet of the West Somerset Foxhounds, which I followed for three hours until rushing on to an 11am meet of the Quantock Staghounds. I spent four hours with this pack, before leaving to travel the short distance to Exford, for a 4pm meet of the Taw Vale Beagles. This pack hunted until 7.30pm, when I was finally able to remove my hard working running boots, which I'd been wearing for the past twelve hours. Then all I had to do was drive the 140 miles back home. Just another day's work, but

About to fly in a Royal Air Force 'Hawk' fast jet trainer on a low level sortie, which had me sweating

Out with the Rockbridge Hunt on one of the coldest days I've ever taken pictures!
Courtesy: Deni McIntyre

that's how it was when I was single-mindedly intent on making a name for myself.

As I've mentioned in previous books, I've always been 'lucky' in life, having survived a broken neck in September 1939, when I fell thirty feet out of a tree. Then, on 1 July 1944 a 'Flying Bomb' blew our house down on top of us, and yet again, on 25 November 1978 when I was kicked in the face by a horse, whilst out with the Tanatside Hunt. Also in sport, where I was ultra competitive, whether playing cricket, or while driving in demolition derbies, or banger racing, I had learned at an early age, that no one remembered who came second.

Perhaps my greatest good fortune is to have a body which has endured the last fifty-three years of physical abuse, brought about by trying to run with hounds, across alien countryside, in many parts of the world. Of course I've pulled muscles, damaged ligaments and put my back 'out' on a regular basis (praise be to chiropractors) but while I've been 'turned out to grass' and told to quit, my body still comes back for more. Nowadays it's a case of 'spirit willing – body trying'! Tremendous changes have taken place in hunting since 1950, where now the lack of money is one reason why there are virtually no second whippers-in, and many kennel-huntsmen are single-handed and try to survive on an agricultural wage, despite having a working week of unlimited hours. At least this ensures that only those with a great love of hounds take the jobs, as nobody does it for the money.

I realise that I am old-fashioned, but I hate to see hunt staff smoking in uniform and feel that, while in scarlet, whippers-in should address their huntsman as Sir. Also, that all followers, on arriving at the meet should ride up to whoever is in charge and say 'Good Morning, Master', something which even I do, although I'm always on foot.

Also, as a very unimportant bystander, I am totally opposed to the recommendation that hunt members and subscribers should NOT wear their traditional scarlet coats as it 'upsets' the antis. I'm certain that the antis would still be 'upset' if people went hunting in loincloths and yellow anoraks, and it would also be damned uncomfortable into the bargain! Here's to many more years of GOOD HUNTING!

Jim Meads
April 2003

Jim Meads at his summer sport banger racing and 'demolition derbies'.

Aiken Hunt, South Carolina, USA
Joint Masters Linda Knox McLean and Eleanor Ward leading the Aiken Hounds through the beautiful colourful Hitchcock Woods in the fall. These woods, comprising 2,200 acres, are among America's largest urban forests, and are much prized and cared for, by those who use them.

The end of a fun day's hunting, with Linda Knox McLean MFH and Eleanor Ward MFH, flanking Namon Corley, who has built and cared for the unique Aiken fences, in the Hitchcock Woods for more than forty-five years.

Albrighton Hunt

Mrs Barbara Perry has been a major force in the Albrighton Hunt for almost fifty years; Joint Master from 1955 to 1992 and President ever since. She is seen here at her ninetieth birthday meet with sons Anthony, Colin and Brian.

Hounds at the double, across old turf, with Garry Williams, Huntsman 1998–2000, on the grey. Since then Garry has hunted the South Notts Hounds most successfully.

Duke of Beaufort's Hunt
Hounds meeting at Badminton House, ancestral home to the Dukes of Beaufort. This is also the setting for the world famous horse trials, which have taken place across the park, since 1949.

Joint Master and Huntsman since 1985 Capt. Ian Farquhar leading hounds and a large mounted field away from an invitation meet at Downton Hall, home of Micky Wiggin, who always has foxes and pheasants on his estate.

Belle Meade Hunt, Georgia, USA
This exciting forward looking hunt has the largest opening meet in the world, with around 130 members following on horses, while 750 others board tally-ho wagons, from which they watch the day's sport. Here they are on the move across country.

Joint Master and Huntsman 'Epp' Wilson, with his high-class pack of cross-bred foxhounds, on the move through one of their country's wooded areas, where foxes and coyotes are found.

Belvoir (Duke of Rutland's) Hunt

An end of season group of Masters and staff, at their historic 18th Century kennels, close to Belvoir Castle. L to R *Martin Thornton – Huntsman, John Martin MFH, Joey Newton MFH, Richard Morley MFH, Sten Bertelsen MFH, Edward Irving – Whipper-in.*

Martin Thornton, Huntsman since 1992, leading his Old English Foxhounds away from a meet at Belvoir Castle, home of The Duke of Rutland, who owns the hounds. This is always the 'end of season' fixture.

Berkeley Hunt

One of the great family packs, where the Masters and staff wear yellow livery. Hounds have been kept at Berkeley since the 12th Century and are here seen in front of Berkeley Castle with Huntsman Chris Maiden, while on exercise.

Even the stables and kennels have a regal air and are seen to advantage in this picture where Major John Berkeley, who owns the hounds exhibits the pack, shown by Huntsman Chris Maiden, to some visitors and Masters.

Blencathra Hunt

Huntsman Barry Todhunter, who took over from the renowned Johnny Richardson in 1988, with hounds, high in the Fells. These hounds are descended from those bred by the legendary huntsman John Peel who died in 1854.

Brecon and Talybont Hunt

A very wet morning as Huntsman Ian Hawkins leads his hounds away from a meet at the 'Barley Mow', in Builth Wells, during the popular hunt week.

Later in the day and a totally different setting, as hounds mark a fox to ground, high on a steep bracken-covered hillside, with their huntsman.

15

Brothers
Anthony Adams,
Huntsman of the
Heythrop since 1987,
with his brother Trevor,
Joint Master and
Huntsman of the Duke of
Buccleuch's since 1989.

The Barbers judging a
Welsh Hound show.
David is Joint Master
and Huntsman of the
Tivyside, while Gary has
carried the horn at the
Pembrokeshire since
1989.

The Nicholson brothers are both professional huntsmen, but of very different hounds. Anthony is with the Derwent, while Michael hunts the Coniston Fell Hounds, in the Lake District, on foot.

An ideal opportunity presented itself to photograph the Hill brothers together in uniform, when their packs held a joint meet. Oliver on the grey, is Joint Master and Huntsman of the United, while Mark is a Joint Master of the Vale of White Horse Hunt.

Calf Pasture Bassets (Maryland) and the Orange County Harehounds (Vermont)

A joint meet of these two American packs, in the Hamilton Hunt country, during the Ontario Festival of Hunting in Canada. In the centre are the two huntsmen 'Jeep' Cochran MBH and Laura Janney MBH.

Hounds walking home at the end of an exhilarating day's hunting. In the centre are the two huntsmen 'Jeep' Cochran MBH and Laura Janney MBH while to the left is our host, Sherry Ballentyne and to the right, with his jacket off, is Steve Clifton, Huntsman to the Eglinton and Caledon Foxhounds.

Casanova Hunt, Virginia, USA

Long serving huntsman Tommy Lee Jones taking his hounds to draw, following a meet at Longwood Farm. He has carried the horn since 1970, with great success.

Truly a sight to set the blood racing! Three lovely ladies riding three super grey hunters, heading the field on a sunny morning, Joyce Fendley MFH, Kay Blassic MFH and Jane Gaston – well known sporting artist.

19

Cattistock Hunt

Huntsman Charlie Watts blowing hounds away, during a hunt in the Dorset hills, close to Sydling St Nicholas. The leading tan coloured hound is one of their most successful American crosses.

The field enjoying a gallop during a hunt on perfect old turf, in the Dorset hills. On the grey (second right) *is Senior Joint Master, The Hon. Charlotte Townshend, who has been in office since 1986.*

College Valley and North Northumberland Hunt

This famous pack was founded in 1924, by Sir Alfred Goodson and Capt. The Hon. Claude Lambton, to hunt foxes on the Scottish borders. For half of the hunt's eighty-year history (1964-2003), Joint Master Martin Letts, here taking the pack to a fresh draw, has carried the horn.

Coops

These are the normal types of jump encountered during a day's hunting in most parts of North America.

Lt. Col. Dennis Foster, Executive Director of the American MFHA, is a widely travelled former MFH and Huntsman, who does a wonderful job in keeping people aware of the antics of those who would have foxhunting banned world-wide.

Diana Rowson is one of a tiny number of professionals who have whipped-in to hounds on three continents: the South Shropshire and the Meynell in England; the Midland in Georgia and Alabama and the Adelaide Hunt Club in Australia.

Jimmy Young is a second generation Master of one of America's most prestigious packs, the Orange County, whose country is very close to Washington DC, yet is delightfully rural.

Airborne over a coop, on a mist filled canyon only twenty miles north west of Los Angeles, is West Hills Hunt Secretary, Kathleen Lorden.

In full flight over a coop are the Masters and Staff of the Belle Meade Hunt in Georgia at their spectacular opening meet.

Enjoying a hunt in Canada is Roger Deslauriers, a Joint Master of the Montreal Hounds since 1992.

Giving a great lead over this coop in the snow, during a hunt with the Glenmore, is Graham Pitsenberger MFH and Field Master. On the grey is Will McIntyre from the Yadkin Valley Hunt.

Clearing a coop, against a colourful panorama of Canadian countryside, is Walter Pady MFH, Toronto and North York Hunt.

Cotswold Hunt

Foxhunting and steeple-chasing have always been closely allied; here, Tim Unwin MFH and Huntsman 1971-99, parades hounds on the hallowed turf of Cheltenham Racecourse, where they always receive a warm welcome from racegoers.

Julian Barnfield, who took over as Huntsman from Tim Unwin MFH in 1999, leading the hunt across lovely open country, at the end of a hunt on Mark Vestey's Foxcote Estate.

North Cotswold Hunt

The early morning sun highlights Joint Master and Huntsman Nigel Peel, as he takes hounds to draw a covert, just before the opening meet, in this delightful little country, with its hills and vale.

Plough and stone walls are much in evidence, as this 'Bitches only' pack with Nigel Peel MFH and Huntsman, head for home. His Joint Master wife Sophia, is heading the ratcatcher dressed field.

Countryside Alliance Meet on The Royal Welsh Showground, at Builth Wells, in January 2001
Official figures gave the number of foot followers as well over 1,000, while the number of horses in the field was 483, making it the biggest meet I've had the pleasure of photographing.

Five packs were invited to bring hounds and here are the Huntsmen (L to R) Will Jones MFH (Irfon & Towy) David Morgan (Radnor & West Hereford) David Jones (David Davies) Ian Hawkins (Brecon & Talybont) Roy Savage (Teme Valley).

Cub-Hunting
The sun just rising above the horizon, to burn off an early morning mist, as the Warwickshire Hounds prepare to draw a covert.

An early morning meet of the Millbrook Hounds, at their kennels in New York State, only twelve days after the ghastly events of 11 September 2001. (L to R) Farnham Collins MFH, Betsy Park – Huntsman since 1978, Richard Verrilli MFH, Nancy Stahl MFH.

Donald Philhower, who has hunted The Golden's Bridge Hounds since 1978, leading his Penn-Marydel pack through a colourful field of Golden Rod, only thirty miles north of New York City.

The Midland Hounds with Joint Master and Huntsman Mason Lampton, at an early morning meet, close to a lake, from which mist is rising. This was an occasion for formal dress, as it was a special meet, held to commemorate Senior Master Ben Hardaway's 80th birthday, in style!

William Wakeham, Joint Master and Huntsman of Sir Watkin Williams-Wynn's Hunt, collecting hounds at the end of a busy morning's cub-hunting.

The United Pack's Joint Master and Huntsman Oliver Hill, taking hounds to draw this delightful, unspoiled country on the Welsh Marches, from an early morning meet at 'The Down'.

Cumberland Farmers Hunt

Hounds meeting at Cowarch, an exotic location in the mountains of mid-Wales, during an exchange visit. A fox was marked to ground in rocky crags, towards the top of the picture, where he was left!

Joint Master and Huntsman Peter Wybergh and his guide, David Jones, Huntsman of the David Davies, leading hounds and field, along a mountain track.

David Davies Hunt
Following the opening meet on 19 October 2002, Huntsman David Jones, in his 30th season with this pack, is pictured on his winning point to pointer 'Metro' against a background of a gorse-covered hill, above the Llandinam Kennels.

This fine pack of Welsh and Fell Foxhounds, wait with Huntsman David Jones and numerous foot followers, after marking a fox to ground, at the end of a twisting hunt in the hills.

Ditches Away
Sir Jonathan Clark
showing fine style as he
leads the Wynnstay field
over a hedge and ditch.

Hon. Secretary to the
Cottesmore Hunt since
1981, Michael Stokes
clears timber and ditch
during a hunt from
Orton Park.

Safely over a big black Cottesmore hedge and ditch is Christopher Smith, enjoying a hunt after the 'four o'clock fox'.

Dominic Gascoine going well, while in pursuit of the Wynnstay Hounds, across their lovely grass country.

Ditches Towards

What a 'buzz' Jane Muskett must have felt as her well-bred hunter met this Cheshire hedge and ditch absolutely right, and effortlessly reached the other side in fine style.

I feel that this picture of the Quorn Hunt Field with Joint Master Richard Carden, in the centre, really captures the 'haroosh' of jumping a hedge and ditch in close company with other horses and riders.

Former Cheshire Hunt Joint Master John Boddington and his athletic grey, in full flight over a big hedge and ditch, which stopped several horses and riders.

Dukes and Duchesses

The 9th Duke of Buccleuch, pictured here when President of the Peterborough Royal Foxhound Show in 1995, has been master of his family pack since 1970, despite being wheelchair bound for many years – the result of a hunting accident.

The Duchess of Rutland (left) with her three daughters, The Ladies Alice, Violet and Eliza, at a meet of The Duke of Rutland's Hounds, at her home, Belvoir Castle.

The Duke and Duchess of Marlborough, who live in the historic Blenheim Palace, hunt regularly with the Heythrop Hounds, which run across the park at Blenheim every season.

BELOW LEFT:
The 11th Duke of Beaufort, who as David Somerset rode in the Badminton Three Day Event, has been Joint Master of the family pack since 1974.

BELOW RIGHT:
The 10th Duke of Beaufort, universally known as 'Master', hunted hounds from 1920-1967 and was Master from 1924-1984.

Eglinton & Caledon Hunt, Canada

Huntsman Steve Clifton and his Whipper-in son Sam, leading a big 'Ontario Festival of Hunting' field across open country, on their way to draw. Just behind hounds are two visiting Huntsmen, Mark Powell, Toronto and North York and Ralph Cole MFH, Bethany Hills-Frontenac Hunt.

Keeping in touch with hounds as they draw an area of thick cover, is Huntsman Steve Clifton, who was at one time, with Jack Champion, at the Old Surrey and Burstow Hunt, near London, UK.

Exmoor Hunt

With the kennels not being suitable for the puppy show, it was held for many years, at Emmett's Grange, home of Hon. Secretary Josh Brown. As a treat for the hounds, they were hacked across the moor to the kennels at Balewater after the show.

With the evening sun highlighting hounds and their white sterns, Tony Wright, Huntsman since 1982, follows his pack through Cornham Ford, on their way home to kennels.

Fall – Glenmore Hunt, Virginia, USA
A last minute stop caused this rider to go 'out the front door', but her landing was softened by the snow!

Fall – Piedmont Hunt, Virginia, USA
This unfortunate rider shows that even a small wall can cause problems when his horse put in a 'dirty' stop in the very last stride. Amazingly, this rider escaped without a single scratch!

Fences.
Whipper-in to the V.W.H. Hunt and moving to the Bicester with Whaddon Chase on 1 May 2003, Gareth Bow in full flight over a wire and timber fence.

Joint Master and Huntsman of the Warwickshire Foxhounds, John Pritchard, gets airborne during a morning's cub-hunting.

43

Hunt Secretary Andrew Spalding jumping a tidy fence, during a misty hunt with the Zetland.

Unusual in that he was at one time a Joint Master of the Cottesmore Hunt and the Quorn, Joss Hanbury MFH, is a very difficult man to follow across country.

Clearing, in fine style, a real 'old fashioned' fence in Co. Durham, during a hunt with the Zetland, is Paul Morrison MFH.

Lady Felicity Blyth, a Joint Master of the Cotswold Hunt and her Appaloosa horse, see a stride and clear this upright fence in fine style.

The Fernie Hunt

The front rank of a 120-strong field jumping timber, as they race away from the famous John Ball covert, near Mowsley. Leading is Charles Millington MFH, while third right is the Field Master Philip Cowen.

With the light fading, Huntsman Derek Hopkins collects his dark coloured hounds, before leading them home, at the end of a grand day's sport, ending on the Laughton Hills with a brace of foxes accounted for.

Field Masters
Showing the way over a neat thorn hedge in Co. Durham, is Zetland Hunt Joint Master, Paul Morrison.

Leading a very orderly Live Oak Hunt Field, through a quail-shooting plantation in Florida, is Mercer Fearington. His wife Katie, is Hunt Secretary.

Adrian Smith, Joint Master of the Ledbury Hunt, giving a good lead over a neatly trimmed thorn hedge, in their vale country.

Chairman Antony Brassey leading a large mounted field of the Duke of Beaufort's Hunt.

Phil Arthers, who has been a Joint Master of the Meynell & South Staffs Hunt since 1990, flying a jump ahead of Billy Foulkes MFH.

'Pinging' a post and rails fence out of a covert, is Pytchley Hunt Joint Master, Richard Spencer.

Friends

What would life be like without friends? It doesn't bear thinking about! Here are two of my best friends together with hounds. Pytchley Huntsman Peter Jones, a lifelong friend, who came to my 50th, 60th and 70th birthday parties. Marion Maggiolo, whom I've only known since 1994, owns 'Horse Country', a fabulous store in Warrenton, Virginia, which publishes its own newspaper, using many of my pictures and stories, and where my last two books have been launched.

Full Cry
Sir Watkin Williams-Wynn's old English type foxhounds, in full cry across a water-logged grazing meadow in their lovely grass country.

The Midland Hounds racing across a stubble field under a threatening sky, during a visit to the Piedmont Country in Virginia.

Glenmore Hunt, Virginia, USA

Although conditions were cold, bleak and inhospitable, the welcome I received at the Glenmore Hunt, was most warming. Here, with snow everywhere, Joint Master Graham Pitsenberger, leads the field to the first draw.

Huntsman Chris Knoedler, who was formerly with the Mells Hunt, leading the way back to the trailers, at the end of a day's sport, in the snow. Behind the pack are Mary O'Brien, Graham Pitsenberger MFH, Col. Hugh Sproul III MFH and Teresa T. Stewart.

Gogerddan Hunt

The original Gogerddan Hunt was formed around 1600 by Sir Richard Pryse and went into abeyance in the 1980s, on the death of Marjorie Lady Pryce MFH. It was re-formed in 1990 by John Charles Jones MFH, seen in the centre of hounds following a meet in the hills above Tregaron, in mid-Wales.

Huntsman Jason Williams pictured with hounds after running a fox to ground in a huge peat bog, seemingly in the middle of nowhere!

Golden Valley Hunt

This pack was formed in 1945, to hunt what was formerly Capt. Hope's country, from 1922-39. Here, hounds, staff and a keen mounted following, meet on a bracken-clad hillside, above the River Wye.

Joint Masters Chris Davies and Elizabeth Thorneycroft, with Robbie Alman, heading the field into the hills, after changing horses.

Green Spring Valley Hunt, Maryland, USA
Andrew Barclay, who hunted these hounds from 1980-2001, having previously whipped-in to Les Grimes, jumping a very upright coop, while taking hounds to draw a covert.

Here, on a very wet day, Andrew Barclay parades his good-looking pack on the Maryland Hunt Cup course, with one of the imposing timber fences, in the background.

Hedges

Caroline Dennis, on her good coloured horse, over a Zetland hedge with an unexpected drop.

'Kiki' Allsopp, who was a Joint Master of the Old Berkshire Hunt 1984-95, is in perfect unison with her horse, as they clear a recently cut, thorn hedge, during a fast hunt.

The elegantly attired Howard Milton and his grand hunter make an excellent picture as they fly a Cotswold hedge above Andoversford.

Sean Frankham over a thorn hedge, during a hunt with the Fernie, on the Laughton Hills.

Mark Dibble clearing a big thorn hedge in full flower, during an end of season hunt in the North Shropshire country.

Grafton Joint Master from 1999-2002, Jenny MacArthur, who writes for The Times *newspaper, over a big thorn hedge, away from Halse Copse.*

Charlotte Banks, who was formerly a top point to point rider, taking a big Albrighton thorn hedge, in her stride.

This cut and laid hedge in the Meynell country, is being jumped by Joint Master Tessa Hibbert.

North Herefordshire Hunt

Long serving Harley Godsall has been with this pack since 1966, carrying the horn since 1980. He is pictured here jumping timber, near to Bredenbury, as he takes hounds to a holloa.

'Keep in close to the hedge' the field were told and that is just what they are doing. Leading the way are two Joint Masters, Gilly Bulmer and Phillip Blackman-Howard, at whose home the meet had been held.

Heythrop Hunt
One of the country's most famous hound breeding packs, are seen in their kennels at Chipping Norton, with Huntsman Anthony Adams, who has been in charge since 1987.

These hounds, which hunt equally as well as they look, are seen here, with huntsman Anthony Adams, drawing a field of roots, on Icomb Hill, during cub-hunting.

Hillsboro Hunt, Tennessee, USA

English Huntsman Johnny Gray and his Whipper-in wife Karen taking his good looking pack of mainly cross-bred foxhounds to draw.

With hounds at the end of a busy day's hunting are Huntsman Johnny Gray, Senior Joint Master Henry Hooker and Bruce P'Pool MFH.

Hound Shows

The first major show of the summer is the South of England, close to London's Gatwick Airport. 2002 was the Queen's Golden Jubilee Year and she toured the Show with Carola Godman Law, in an open horse draw carriage, to tremendous cheers.

The Wales and Border Counties show at Builth Wells, is the Welsh equivalent of Peterborough, as the show which everyone dreams of winning. Here is the final line up in the class for couples of entered bitches, shown by their huntsmen, on bended knee, as is the Welsh fashion.

The Great Yorkshire Show at Harrogate, is one of only two which are held indoors. This picture shows the bitch championship being judged by Ian McKie MFH and Mark Hankinson MFH. Hunt staff in the ring are Anthony Adams (Heythrop) with the winner 'Poplin', Peter McColgan (Middleton) and Sandy Wilson (Morpeth).

The mecca for hunting people in the summer, is the Peterborough Royal Foxhound Show, where the amphitheatre-like ring becomes so heavily charged with atmosphere during judging. Here the class for couples of unentered bitches comes under scrutiny.

The little Devon town of Honiton, provides the setting for the West of England Hound show. Often established winners are beaten and I have seen Peterborough Champions relegated to the lower echelons in big classes. This picture illustrates the ring, filled with the always exciting class for two couples of entered bitches.

Lowther Show is unique in that, from all the hounds entered, be they foxhounds, harriers or beagles one is chosen as the Supreme Champion. Then as a grand finale, comes a huge parade of hounds, in the main ring, in front of an enthusiastic audience.

Set amongst the most glorious
scenery in the Lake District, near
to Ambleside, Rydal Show is run
in conjunction with sheep dog
trials, while the foxhound classes
are only open to the six fell packs.
Here, on the flagstones are the
Huntsmen of these six packs
(L to R) *Edmund Porter MFH
(Eskdale & Ennerdale), John
Harrison (Ullswater), Michael
Nicholson (Coniston), 'Pritch'
Bland (Melbreak), Barry
Todhunter (Blencathra), and Paul
Whitehead (Lunesdale).*

Something different takes place at
the Virginia Hound Show, where,
in addition to the normal classes,
they have pack classes. These are
quite similar to an obedience test,
where the huntsman runs and
manoeuvres five couples of
hounds, in front of two judges.
Here, Robert Dougherty MFH
(Plum Run) wins with his Old
English Foxhounds.

Hound Trials

In recent times, hound trials have become a very popular part of the American foxhunting scene, drawing large crowds in the southern states. So far, only Frank Houghton Brown MFH (Middleton) has been far sighted enough to organise them in the U.K. This picture shows Belvoir huntsman Martin Thornton collecting hounds from six invited packs, at the end of the Trial's second day.

Waiting to add up the scores of each hound, before announcing the results, are these extremely knowledgeable judges (L to R) *William Wakeham MFH (Sir Watkin Williams-Wynn's), Alastair Jackson (Director of the M.F.H.A.), Frank Houghton Brown MFH (Middleton) and Trials Organiser, Martin Thornton (Belvoir Huntsman complete with foxes' brush), David Jones (David Davies, Huntsman), Adrian Dangar, Martin Letts MFH (College Valley) and The Hon. Nick Crossley.*

Hunt Fields
United Pack Joint Master Robert George, who is used to field mastering twenty riders found himself in charge of 110, when the V.W.H. Hounds paid his Hunt a visit!

Five followers of the Gogerddan Hunt in a variety of clothing, passing one of the Welsh reservoirs at Ffair-Rhos near Tregaron.

Heading a large field of the Ottawa Valley Hunt during the 'Ontario Festival of Hunting' are (L to R), Gus Schickedanz MFH (Eglinton and Caledon), Seymour Epstein (Host for meet), Walter Pady MFH (Toronto & N York), Ted Thomas MFH and Kay Leach MFH both Ottawa Valley.

With steam rising from sweating horses, the Pytchley field checks during a fast hunt from a meet at Thornby House in Northamptonshire.

Followers of the Cotswold Hunt bunch up, as hounds hit off the line, after a check.

With the early morning sun beginning to clear an overnight mist, followers of the South Creek Hunt in Florida, move through some unusual vegetation to watch hounds hunt a grey fox.

With a marvellous background of mid-Wales countryside, Lord Davies, Master of the David Davies Hunt since 1963, has some of his field gathered around him, as they watch hounds work.

A big field of The Duke of Buccleuch's Hunt, on the move across lovely old turf in Scotland.

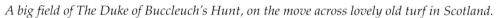

Winter sunshine lights up the followers of the College Valley and North Northumberland Hunt, on a day when hounds hunted in England and Scotland.

The field of the Kilmoganny Hunt in Ireland, sensibly dressed to keep out the incessant and penetrating rain.

Ireland – A look back

Since making my debut in Ireland in 1962, I have had many wonderful days in the hunting field, where a huge variety of obstacles are encountered. However, I also recall some splendid occasions at the Dublin Horse show, including the Co. Down Staghounds and their Master from 1962–75 Tom Moore, jumping the famous Irish bank, in the Ballsbridge Arena.

Capt. Brian Fanshawe showed great sport at the Galway Blazers during his Mastership from 1969-72, when I often stayed at The Craughwell Kennels, with Brian and his wife Libby. In this picture the black clouds led to a blizzard as hounds wait with their huntsman.

Just looking at this picture of Huntsman Hugh Robards and his Old English foxhounds of the County Limerick Hunt marking to ground is enough to send shivers down my back. It was a day of continuous, freezing rain, yet Lord (Toby) Daresbury MFH was determined to give the mounted field a full day's sport, and wouldn't give the order to go home until dusk.

Leading hounds along a wall comprising huge stones, with a typical Irish bog on the far side is John Smith, who was part of the Westmeath Hunt scene for many years. Arriving in 1964, as Kennel-Huntsman to Lt. Col. Dennis Purdon, John became huntsman in 1966, continuing to carry the horn as a professional and also as a Joint Master from 1985 until his retirement in 1993.

In 1963, Capt. Harry Freeman-Jackson, Joint Master and Huntsman of the Duhallow Hounds, won the Burghley Three Day Event, on 'St Finbarr'. This photo was taken that same season and shows Capt. Freeman-Jackson (on the left) and his long serving kennel-huntsman Harry Clayton, leading hounds from a meet in a typical Co. Cork village.

Michael Higgens MFH, who hunted the Tipperary Hounds from 1973-91, had a most amazing record in this fearsome bank and ditch grass country. Despite carrying the horn on well over 2000 occasions, he never missed a single day which says much for his riding ability and his strong constitution, which enabled him to carry on through thick and thin.

Irfon and Towy Hunt

This is one of the few packs which are still composed entirely of pure Welsh foxhounds – so many others have brought in fell hounds and run them together. Although I am English, I have a soft spot for Welsh hounds, and really enjoy watching and listening to them hunt.

With hounds on their way to a meet at the 'Barley Mow', Builth Wells, where the group picture was taken, are the two Joint Masters. Ken Jones (on the left) and his family have a long association with this pack, which was formed in 1909, while Will Jones, who has hunted hounds since 1983, has the kennels at his farm.

Iroquois Hunt, Kentucky, USA
With hounds hunting in the snow, from a meet at the Corners, is Joint Master and Huntsman Jerry Miller, who has many top English blood lines in his kennels, on Grimes Mill Road, Lexington.

Lilla Mason, who shares the duties of Huntsman with Jerry Miller MFH, collecting hounds at the end of a hunt.

Mr Jefford's Hounds, Wyoming, USA

I encountered some of the most spectacular scenery of my hunting career when I travelled to Iron Mountain, Wyoming, to photograph these Penn-Marydell Hounds. Huntsman Martyn Blackmore here leads hounds past a lake reflecting the azure blue sky, while drawing for a coyote.

Unbelievable though it sounds, when I photographed these black and tan hounds moving through an area of red soil and rocks, I was 7,000 feet above sea-level and the temperature nudging upwards towards 90°F; luckily humidity was low!

Jumping for Joy!

Caught in mid-air while jumping a big stone wall, high up a mountain in Snowdonia, in company with a terrier and foxhounds, is Richard Williams, Master and owner of the Eryri Hounds. Behind the wall is former Royal Rock Beagles Huntsman and noted terrier breeder John Broadhurst, who now lives in North Carolina.

Horse, rider and hounds, all having fun during a hunt in Florida, with the Misty Morning. Leading is Alexis Macaulay, Joint Master and Huntsman, with the temperature in the high 70s!

Kennel Work

An old huntsman's proverb says that 'Foxes are caught in the kennels'! By this they meant that good kennel management and feeding produced healthy, happy and fit hounds, which were able to hunt well enough to catch foxes. Here Michael Rowson is at work in the South Shropshire Hunt Kennels, where he was in charge from 1968-2002.

South Shropshire foxhound puppies are pictured here, eating raw meat, which had been carefully prepared by the hunt staff. This had been collected from local farms, as fallen stock.

East Kent Hunt

This Hunt is lucky in that it has enjoyed that much-needed ingredient, continuity. Here are two who have contributed to this happy state of affairs, riding together on a day 'stolen' from the snowy weather. Mr Reg Older was an extremely popular master from 1967–97, while Richard Blakeney has carried the horn with much success since 1976.

Here, Richard Blakeney takes his good-looking pack of modern English Foxhounds, to draw a covert, with snow drifts still in evidence, along a fence line.

81

Ladies in Scarlet

Looking good over a coop in rugged terrain in California, is the Santa Fe Hunt's professional Kennelman Brooke Rogers.

Gina Salatino leading the Why Worry Hunt followers along a leafy trail through a wood in South Carolina.

Former Master and now Amateur Whipper-in to the Albrighton Woodland Hunt, Natasha Wheeler is also a regular competitor in horse trials.

Not only is Kerrie Hayes the daughter of Rose Tree Hunt Master and Huntsman Jody Murtagh, but she is also Field Master.

Taking The Edisto-Mount Vintage Hounds to draw, near to their kennels in South Carolina, is Joint Master and Huntsman 'D.K.' Cheatham Newell. Close behind is her young son Walter, who whips-in.

Jumping a tree trunk amidst exotic foliage in Florida is the Misty Morning Hunt's Field Master, Cindy Thyberg.

Senior Master since 1983, of the Plum Run Hunt in Pennsylvania, Suzy Reingold has the only pack of Old English Foxhounds, in America.

Emma Powell, who whips in to her husband Mark, at the Toronto and North York Hunt in Canada, jumping out of a colourful covert during the autumn. She gave birth to their son Glyn Jim, ten weeks later!

Liberty and Livelihood March – 2002

Part of a large contingent from the Ludlow Hunt, including Capt. Rupert Inglesant MFH and Huntsman (left) and enthusiastic junior members

Huge crowds of marchers, packing the streets in London's west end, including senior citizens and children on their parents' shoulders.

Already almost 200,000 people had marched under the counting archway, in Whitehall, with more than that number still to come.

'Stars and Stripes' flying on Westminster Bridge with Big Ben and the Houses of Parliament behind. With the flags are some of our many American foxhunting friends who crossed the Atlantic Ocean to show their support. (R to L) Marty Wood MFH (Live Oak), Daphne Wood MFH (Live Oak), Carol Anne Morley (Wentworth), Penny Denegre MFH (Middleburg), Pat Rogers (Middleburg) and Brent Concilio (North Country).

Live Oak Hunt, Florida, USA

Founder Master of the Hunt in 1974, Marty Wood III pictured here with his good looking pack of English and cross-bred foxhounds, now shares the duties of huntsman with his professional Charles Montgomery.

With hounds at the end of a hunt, which finished on freshly burned ground, on a quail plantation, are the Joint Masters, Marty and Daphne Wood III.

With hounds marking a red fox to ground in a tangled mass of very sharp thorns, is huntsman Charles Montgomery.

Huntsman Charles Montgomery and Whipper-in Dale Barnett, leading hounds back to kennels after a most successful day's hunting. In the background is 'Live Oak', home of the Joint Masters, Marty and Daphne Wood III.

Ludlow Hunt

With the lovely Downton Hall Estate in the background, Joint Master and Huntsman Capt. Rupert Inglesant, taking his English and Welsh cross hounds to draw after changing horses.

Capt. Rupert Inglesant Joint Master and Huntsman of this pack on the Welsh Marches, leading hounds through a stream at the end of a hunt.

Lunesdale Hunt

Being huntsman to one of the fell packs of the Lake District, is a desperately hard life, as all hunting is conducted on foot, on three or four days per week. The fells are steep and take much climbing, even when the weather is good. Here, Paul Whitehead has just unboxed his hounds at the meet, following an overnight fall of snow, which made the going slippery.

However, it takes more than a fall of snow to deter those who follow the fell hounds, as this picture shows. The huntsman's red coat is just visible high up the steep slope, as followers endeavour to scale the heights.

Marren Bloodhounds

Andrew Marren, who founded this pack in Shropshire at the age of nineteen is Master and Huntsman and lives for hunting.

The end of a hunt, as the hounds catch up with their 'clean boot' quarry. This active young lady is 'Mouse' Coakley, girl-friend of the Master and Huntsman Andrew Marren, who is watching!

Meets

With the Towy and Cothi Hounds meeting in a Welsh farmyard, is Dewi Price, their huntsman for the past 30 seasons.

This lawn meet at Forcett Barns provided a dilemma for the Zetland Masters, 'Would the fog clear'! Yes it did! (L to R) Carolyn Cameron, MFH and Jamie Cameron – Hosts, David Jukes – Huntsman, Matthew Tunmore – Whipper-in, Paul Morrison, MFH.

The last ever meet of the North Warwickshire Hunt was held on 23 March 1985 at Hatton House, home of Capt. 'Pup' Arkwright (right) for many years a Joint Master. Here with hounds are (L to R) Brian Charley, MFH – Wendy Evans, MFH – Micky Wills (Whipper-in) Ivor Bunch (Huntsman) Mary Way MFH.

Among the top packs in Wales, the David Davies hunt on horses at weekends, and on foot for the rest of the time. Here is a typical meet, at a turkey farm, where among the gathered masses of all ages, is a noted visitor, Lt. Col. Dennis Foster, Executive director of the American M.F.H.A.

Itton Court near Chepstow, is famous in the annals of hound breeding, for it was the home of Sir Edward Curre MFH 1896–1930, who bred the 'White Hounds of Itton'. These were crossed extensively with English bitches, thus improving the breed. This picture shows a joint meet of the Curre Hounds and the Berkeley Hounds, whose masters and staff are wearing their distinctive yellow livery.

Another meet with a difference, is the opening meet of the Misty Morning Hounds, in Ocala, Florida on an appropriately 'misty morning'. Hounds are being blessed by The Rev. Charles Peyton, who is close to the Scottish pipers and drummer, who provided the music. Joint Master and Huntsman Alexis Macaulay is in the foreground.

95

The North Staffordshire Hunt, with their dark coloured, Old English Hounds, meeting at Oakley Hall near Market Drayton, in the rain.

Numbers attending this meet of the Belle Meade Hunt in Georgia, USA, were swollen by the presence of the Directors of The American M.F.H.A., seen here on their horses, standing behind hounds, grouped around 'Epp' Wilson MFH.

Midland Hunt, Georgia, Alabama, USA

Following his exciting and successful pack of hounds through a creek is Joint Master and Huntsman Mason Lampton. Not only is he 1st Vice President of The American M.F.H.A. but also a son-in-law of the Senior Master, Ben Hardaway, who started this hunt in 1950.

Ben Hardaway MFH since 1950 and huntsman for much of that time, celebrated his 80th birthday with a tremendous party and a day's hunting. Here is the 'end of day' picture, showing Ben with a coyote caught after a 'race' of fifty-five minutes. With him is huntsman Mark Dixon and holding his sweaty grey hunter Whipper-in Robert Miller.

Millennium Day – 1 January 2000

On the first day of the New Millennium, the Pytchley Hunt met at West Haddon Hall, to be greeted by this awesome banner, draped across the front of the house.

The four Joint Masters of the Pytchley Hunt at the meet at West Haddon Hall (L to R) Michael Bletsoe-Brown, Joan Tice, Richard Spencer, Edwin Baker.

Misty Morning Hounds, Florida, USA

With a typical Florida background, Joint Master and Huntsman Alexis Macaulay signals the end of a hunt, as hounds gather around with the temperature above 80°F.

Mooreland Hunt, Alabama, USA

Huntsman Randy Waterman, leading hounds away from an invitation meet in the Live Oak Hunt Country in Florida with Marty Wood III MFH and Huntsman of the Live Oak.

The end of a seventy-five minute 'race' after a black coyote, following an invitation meet in the Live Oak country. (L to R) Dr Jack Sewell, MFH, Randy Waterman, Huntsman, Dr Jon Moody, MFH, Leslie Rhett Crosby, MFH (all Mooreland). Daphne Wood, MFH, Marty Wood MFH and Huntsman, Charles Montgomery, Huntsman, Dale Barnett, Whipper-in (all Live Oak).

Nostalgia
The 1958 opening meet of the Taunton Vale Foxhounds at Jordans. With hounds are Joint Master and Huntsman Alan Fletcher, and Jim Bailey, long serving Kennel-Huntsman or Huntsman.

Leading the Old Berkeley Hounds to draw, across acres of plough in 1969, is long serving Huntsman Jim Bennett and Whipper-in Harry Barber.

A member of a famous family of hunt servants, Jack Champion was Huntsman of the Old Surrey and Burstow Hounds, on London's south eastern doorstep from 1947–85.

The South Oxfordshire Hounds moving along a muddy lane in 1965, with Huntsman Tony Younghusband, who later went on to hunt the Bicester.

Harvey Andrews, who hunted the Cowdray Foxhounds from 1954–65, seen here in 1957, on plough, close to the kennels in Cowdray Park, Sussex.

Now the Director of the M.F.H.A. Alastair Jackson is pictured during his last season with the South Dorset where he was Joint Master and Huntsman 1969–80.

103

One of the all-time 'Greats' of foxhunting, Capt. Ronnie Wallace MFH and Huntsman of the Heythrop Hounds from 1952–77, about to put them in to draw a covert, on a damp and misty morning.

A huge joint meet, between the Duke of Beaufort's and the Berkeley Hounds, took place at Badminton on 5 April 1980, to celebrate 'Master's' 80th Birthday. Hounds are seen arriving with their Huntsmen Brian Gupwell and Tim Langley, while behind are some of the 400 plus mounted field and hundreds of motor cars.

The White West Country Harriers of the Dart Vale and Haldon Pack, being taken to draw in Devon in 1963, by Huntsman Sonny Tribble.

For sentimental reasons, I am including this picture of Bill Read, Joint Master and Huntsman of the Amwell Valley Hounds in New Jersey, as this pack was the first one I went out with in America in the mid 1970s. Now in 2003, I have photographed more than eighty different packs of hounds in North America.

Jacqueline Kennedy Onassis, America's former First Lady and a most ardent foxhunter, riding with Charles Whitehouse MFH Orange County, during a day with the Piedmont Hunt, in Virginia.

In 1978, I first had the pleasure of visiting the Midland Hunt in Georgia, where I met its larger than life founder Master and Huntsman, Ben Hardaway III, in office since 1950. It wasn't long before my camera was in action recording Ben exercising hounds, with his Kennel-Huntsman 'Tot' Goodwin now a Joint Master and Huntsman of the Green Creek Hounds, in North Carolina.

With the Joint Masters, Major Robin Fulton (Huntsman) and Michael Close leading the way, the comparatively short lived Bisley and Sandhurst Hounds, leave a meet on their way to draw a covert.

The Devon and Somerset Staghounds, making their way back to kennels with Dennis Boyles, their Huntsman from 1971–91, after taking their stag in Badgworthy Water on Exmoor.

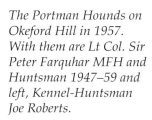

Kennel-Huntsman Bert Taylor, leading the Badsworth Hounds along a track through a wood in Yorkshire, following a meet at Notton, on 5 February 1970.

The Portman Hounds on Okeford Hill in 1957. With them are Lt Col. Sir Peter Farquhar MFH and Huntsman 1947–59 and left, Kennel-Huntsman Joe Roberts.

Leading the Sinnington Hounds on a sparkling winter's morning in North Yorkshire are two of the Joint Masters. The Countess of Feversham, who rode sidesaddle so elegantly, was in office from 1950–85, while Lord Westbury joined her from 1966–74, during which time he hunted hounds.

Mr Goschen's Hunt was formed in 1965 and was operational for some twenty-five years. Their country was in Surrey, Berkshire and Hampshire and this picture shows their professional huntsman Ted Rafton, with hounds drawing a bracken-covered hillside.

Very few people have been a Master of Foxhounds with the same pack for fifty seasons, yet Capt. Charles Barclay, here with hounds on typical plough, held office at the Puckeridge from 1947–2002. He also carried the horn for a great number of years.

With the Hertfordshire Foxhounds, during a morning's cub-hunting, is Master and Huntsman Pat Escombe. In 1970, this pack, together with the Old Berkeley and South Oxfordshire, were amalgamated, to form the Vale of Aylesbury Hunt.

Huntsman Harry Goddard, who was with the Enfield Chace Hunt close to London's northern boundary from 1952–75, leading hounds from an opening meet at Woolmers Park. Behind the pack are Ralph Richardson MFH 1962–77 and Major F Russell-Dore who was a founder Master 1935–45 and 1949–62.

Col. Sir Ralph Carr-Ellison, who was a Master of the West Percy Hunt from 1950–90, pictured against a marvellous background of wild Northumberland countryside, when he was hunting hounds from a meet at Great Ryle in 1970.

Oak Ridge Fox Hunt, Virginia, USA

What spectacular weather in Central Virginia on 7 December 2002. Deep snow, with the temperature a low 15°F, yet the Oak Ridge didn't cancel. Here, Master and Huntsman Rita Mae Brown, leads her hounds to the meet with Whipper-in Dana Flaherty and Ann Marie Gathright, helping out.

Setting out on point duty are professional Whipper-in Dana Flaherty and her amateur counterpart, Mary O'Brien. In the background are the impressive Blue Ridge Mountains.

Master and Huntsman Rita Mae Brown, on her good coloured horse, casts hounds where they had checked in the snow and they begin to run on again.

A snow covered landscape, as Field Master Cindy Chandler and Will McIntyre, lead the way to another covert, during a day with the Oak Ridge Fox Hunt in Central Virginia.

Otter Hounds

The final years of the Border Counties Pack will forever be associated with Joint Master and Huntsman Ray Williams, latterly with his wife Jackie. Ray, seen here casting hounds across the River Severn, also founded and hunted the Wyre Forest Beagles in 1947.

The imposing Downton Castle dominates the skyline, as the Hawkstone pack gather, ready to begin a day on the River Teme. With hounds is Joint Master and Huntsman Michael Downes, while to the left, is long serving kennel huntsman Jack Stallard.

With the amalgamation of the Bucks and Courtenay Tracy Hunts, the new pack had a huge country to cover. This group, pausing on a bridge during a day in the Courtenay Tracy area, includes Huntsman Jeff Hall; Whipper-in Chris Ogilvie; and Joint Masters Mr Sanders and Mrs Van Der Kiste.

What a fascinating scene, as the Culmstock Otterhounds meet outside a pretty thatched cottage, in June 1973. With hounds are (L to R) David Allibone; Charlie Mott; Master and Huntsman Norman Bartlett and Anthony Allibone, who has hunted the Dulverton Farmers Foxhounds since 1993.

South Pembrokeshire Hunt

This Hunt has for many years been associated with the Allen family. In 1942 Auriol Allen became Master and this amazing lady remained in office until 1988, when she became President, until her death in 1992; her son Hugh Harrison-Allen, is now Master. Here with very muddy hounds, against a backcloth of Carmarthen Bay, is John Chapple, Huntsman 1958–87.

With hounds on the mudflats of the River Cleddau Estuary at Landshipping are (L to R) Hugh Harrison-Allen MFH, James Andrews MFH and Huntsman Matthew Hickmott, Kennel-Huntsman.

Peterborough Royal Foxhound Show 2001
The secretary's office and cloakrooms were cut off by floodwater after torrential rain, which lasted for much of the day.

Showing just how bad conditions were; here Thurlow Kennel-Huntsman Chris Amatt and Whipper-in Adrian Robinson, lead a couple of hounds to the collecting ring, ready to be judged.

2001 was my fifty-fifth visit to this famous show and never before had I encountered such wet conditions. Here the collecting ring is under water as hunt staff wait to be called to show their hounds.

This year was also notable, as it was the first occasion on which an American MFH had judged foxhounds at Peterborough. Here, that Master, Marty Wood III from the Live Oak Hunt in Florida, is sorting couples of doghounds with David Palmer MFH (Worcestershire) his co-judge.

Plas Machynlleth Hunt

Plas Machynlleth Huntsman Ken Markham, on the edge of a precipitous cliff face, as he watches his hounds hunting hundreds of feet below. Not the place for anyone who suffers from vertigo!

Plum Run Hunt, Pennsylvania, USA
The only pack of Old English Foxhounds in the USA, here with Joint Master and Huntsman Robert Dougherty, on the move through a covert with much undergrowth and a carpet of fallen leaves. As you might guess there was very little scent!

HRH The Prince of Wales
In full flight over a natural hedge, in the Quorn Monday country. The blue stakes show where the electric fencing had been taken down.

Heading the Quorn field near the end of a day in the Hickling area. With the Prince is Nicky Hanbury (wife of MFH) while behind are two of the Joint Masters, Richard Carden and Charles Geary.

Jumping a fence at Ella's Gorse, during a day in the Quorn country.

Over a strongly built hunt jump near to Ab Kettleby, while enjoying a hunt with the Belvoir's Old English Bitch Pack.

Puppy Shows

At least the umbrellas look pretty, as Martin Letts MFH (College Valley) and Simon Hart, judge the Bicester with Whaddon Chase Young Entry in the pouring rain, typical of summer 2002. Showing hounds, at the Stratton Audley Kennels, is Huntsman Patrick Martin.

One of England's most senior professional huntsmen, Jim Lang, has hunted the Burton Hounds since 1967. This Puppy Show in 1999, was a special one, as it marked the retirement from the Mastership of Arthur Lockwood, who was appointed in 1959. His son, John, is now the Senior Joint Master, while his father was MFH 1948-56.

The Cottesmore Young Entry being shown by Huntsman Neil Coleman, to the judges John Lockwood MFH (Burton) and Woodland Pytchley Huntsman Tim Taylor. The walled yard is part of the large Victorian kennels at Ashwell, near Oakham in Rutland.

This is a most unusual puppy show picture, as it catches the very moment that the judges Mark Hankinson MFH (Wilton) and Andrew Cook MFH (South Shropshire) asked United Pack Joint Master and Huntsman Oliver Hill, to instruct his young bitches to jump out of the show ring, into a grassy paddock beyond.

Qualifying Point to Pointers

How nice it was to see champion point to point rider Julian Pritchard, hunting a young point to point prospect properly, not just staying at the back of the field, but by jumping thorn hedges, during a day with the Ledbury.

Champion lady point to point rider, Polly Gundry, in action with the Cattistock Hunt, in Dorset. Both Polly's parents have been Masters of Foxhounds, so she is bred to the job.

Quality Hounds
I've selected four champion doghounds, three from Peterborough whose names now appear in the most prestigious pedigrees, and one from the Virginia Foxhound Show, who is just beginning to make a name for himself.

Peterborough Champion 1990 – Exmoor 'Daresbury'

Peterborough Champion 1992 – Beaufort 'Mostyn'

Peterborough Champion 1993 – Heythrop 'Glazier'
How well I remember trying to photograph 'Glazier', after he had won the Championship. He had an unusual habit; he barked frequently, but every time he did so, he lifted a front leg, making my life very difficult indeed!

Virginia Hound Show Champion 2001 – Live Oak 'Pinecone'
Massive celebrations began at the Show and concluded with a champagne party in The Red Fox Inn, Middleburg. One of 'Pinecone's' dog hound puppies 'Pageboy', won the Open Unentered class in Virginia 2002 – the first of many?

The Queen Mother

This lovely lady, who was revered by everyone, was a great supporter of country sports, including foxhunting, as these pictures, taken at the Peterborough Royal Foxhound Show, well illustrate. Here, the Queen Mother is being escorted by long serving Show Secretary Roy Bird, while following, is Ken Goschen MFH Show President in 1983.

Crawley and Horsham Huntsman Dick Chapman, showing hounds in front of the Royal Box, where the Queen Mother is seated between The Duke of Beaufort MFH and Ken Goschen MFH.

127

Show President in 1992, Sir Watkin Williams-Wynn MFH, about to introduce the Royal guest to South Notts Huntsman Phillip Watts. Behind, is Sir Philip Naylor-Leyland MFH, Chairman of the Show Committee.

The Queen Mother in the Royal Box with Countess Fitzwilliam and Sir Watkin Williams-Wynn MFH, where she took a keen interest in the judging.

Rockbridge Hunt, Virginia, USA

Having safely negotiated the terribly icy lane from the kennels Huntsman David Conner prepares to put hounds into a covert at the start of the day. Following the pack are Kath Conner; Joe Conner and Cindy Morton MFH.

Some of the field watching as hounds hunt through a deep wooded valley way below. Although the temperature was around 28°F, it was the bitterly cold wind which caused the pain!

Rose Tree Fox-Hunting Club, Pennsylvania, USA
Master and Huntsman Jody Murtagh, collecting his pack of Penn-Marydel Hounds at the conclusion of a woodland hunt, during a visit to Canada. With him is Susan Orsini, Joint Master of The Stone Valley Hunt, in New York State.

The Royal Rock Beagles

The Royal Rock Beagles were established in 1845 and have the distinction of being the oldest pack of beagles in the country. They are also one of only a small number where the huntsman wears a scarlet coat. Here, Master and Huntsman Peter Jones looses hounds off through a stream, at the start of the day.

Later that day, which was in a very hilly and open area, hounds are seen hunting through a boggy place, full of rushes, in pursuit of a strong running hare.

131

The Ryeford Chase Griffon Vendeen Hounds

This unique pack of hounds is owned and hunted by the Master, Nick Valentine, a former professional huntsman of the Cotswold Vale Farmers Foxhounds. As well as the 15-inch bassets, Nick also includes in his pack, several couple of working wire-haired dachshunds, and both types can be seen in this picture, as they move to a fresh covert.

Later that same day the heavens opened and we were all soaked, but Nick and his hounds, which have great voices carried on hunting, catching four more well hunted rabbits, before we stopped for a much needed hunt tea.

Sandhurst and Aldershot Beagles

With their home country suffering from an explosion of houses and roads, an early season visit to mid-Wales comes as something of a relief. Here, Huntsman David Greenwood is on hand to help his good looking pack, which included Harrogate Champion 'Brazen', when they checked among an area of rushes.

Standing on a hilltop, against a background of the most magnificent scenery, are two of the Joint Masters, Major Mike McRitchie and Ian Ewart obviously enjoying themselves.

133

Santa Fe Hunt, California, USA

Approaching the meeting place on the Garner Ranch in thick mist, my driver assured me that it would be clear by 9am, and so it proved. As nature unfurled her beauty in front of my eyes I found it difficult to comprehend what I was seeing, so pleasurable was the scene. By the time Terry Paine MFH and his hounds gathered, with the staff and mounted followers, some 5,000 feet above sea level, I knew that I would have a very special picture and here it is!

Field Master Larry Byers leading the mounted field along a canyon floor, with rocky scenery behind and some 5,000 feet above sea level.

Master and Huntsman Terry Paine, with hounds drawing for a coyote, through a flat area dotted with sage brush. Three were hunted well during the day, but all eventually headed for the mountains, where it is impossible to follow, so hounds had to be stopped.

Jumping a coop during the first hunt of the day is Master and Huntsman Terry Paine. This area was once lush grazing land, but a series of droughts has left the grass sun-burned and brown.

Santa Ynez Valley Hunt, California, USA

With an early morning mist slowly clearing, English Huntsman Martyn Blackmore brings his hounds out of a thick covert, before moving on to a fresh draw. This was a day hunting on the Senior Master Steve Lyons' ranch at Los Alamos, in an area where there are many vineyards.

Descending a seriously steep hill, on their way back to kennels as the temperature rises, hounds are with Huntsman Martyn Blackmore and (right) visiting West Hills Master, Mitch Jacobs, MFH.

The Scarteen (Black and Tans)

I was unsure whether to use these two pictures under the heading of 'Scarteen' or 'Record Breakers', because of both characters' ultra long association with this famous Irish hunt. The Ryan family of Scarteen have owned and hunted these black and tan hounds for well over 230 years with Thady Ryan, seen taking them to draw, being appointed Master and Huntsman in 1946. He is still a Joint Master, although now living in New Zealand, with his son Chris carrying the horn.

In 1952 Tommy O'Dwyer was made Kennel-Huntsman and First Whipper-In to the Scarteen Hounds, succeeding his father Jack who had held that post for thirty years. Despite the hazards encountered while crossing this wild, stone wall and bank and ditch country two or three days a week, Tommy was still going strong in the 2002–03 season; some record!

137

Scotland – The Brave

At the beginning of the 2002–03 season, foxhunting as we know it was banned in Scotland, where it has been a traditional country sport for more than 200 years. The Duke of Buccleuch's Hunt dates back to 1827 and here Joint Master and Huntsman Trevor Adams leads hounds and the spread out field, across lovely open grass country, with the Eildon Hills behind.

There has been fox hunting in Dumfriesshire since at least 1816, with one of the early Masters being the 8th Marquis of Queensberry. In 1921 Sir John Buchanan-Jardine became Master and set about breeding what turned out to be this unique pack of big, black and tan hounds. His son, Sir Rupert, is pictured taking them to draw during an early season hunt.

In Fife, out in the east of the country, the foxhounds here have been going since 1786, hunting the land between the Firths of Forth and Tay. For the past fifty years, the Fife hounds have become synonymous with the Gilmour family. Firstly Sir John and, since 1973, his son John, who is seen here with hounds, on the shore of the Loch at Lindores, before going to draw Dunbog.

Out on the west coast of Ayrshire, is a pretty but wet, grass country, where the Eglinton have hunted foxes since 1861, when the 14th Earl of Eglinton was Master. In more recent times, one of foxhunting's great characters, the Hon. Bobby Corbett, was in charge with hounds being hunted from 1972-94, by Guy Sanderson, seen leading his pack across typical old turf.

In August 2002, despite the ban on hunting in Scotland, three of the packs showed hounds at Lowther, to great applause from a large crowd. During a break, I was able to gather together the three huntsmen; Rory Innes MFH (Jed Forest) Richard Holman-Baird MFH (Kincardineshire) and David Barnett (Fife) while in the background, is the kilt-clad Derek Davidson, who held the Fife hounds, in the show ring.

The smallest of the Scottish hunt countries, is the Jed Forest, which passed its centenary in 1984. They have had a couple of real characters in the Mastership in recent years, in Roly Harker 1949–78 and Walter Jeffrey 1983–2000. My picture shows the whole hunt, including staff, hounds and followers, in lovely grass and hill country, after a fourteen mile hunt, to ground.

Side-Saddle

Mary Holt, one of a very small number of ladies riding side-saddle, especially in High Leicestershire, jumps some solid timber, in the Cottesmore country.

Purposefully attacking a timber fence into a rather dark Ludlow hunt covert, is Nicola Roberts.

Snow

As scenic hunting pictures go, this is one of my favourites. It has a marvellous background which the snow enhances, while the horse and rider are jumping as one. I'm certain that Teresa T. Stewart will be pleased with her performance while out with the Glenmore Hunt.

Stowe School is an amazing place for turning out Master of foxhounds. In recent years the following young men have learned their trade by hunting the Stowe Beagles: Tom Bannister; Frank Houghton Brown; Adrian Dangar; Adam Waugh; Richard Tyacke and Charles Frampton. In this wintery picture Master and Huntsman Rob Oliver is leading hounds from a meet at Evenley.

North Staffordshire Hunt

Huntsman Barry Cox leading hounds away from a lawn meet at Oakley Hall, for what turned out to be an action packed day with much jumping. Note the dark coloured, Old English Foxhounds.

With the ground showing much evidence of torrential overnight rain, the field watch as hounds draw a covert, which held a fox that gave a decent hunt.

The Stoke Hill Beagles

Although their country is in the west of England, each year the Stoke Hill Beagles pay a visit to mid-Wales, where they hunt some seriously steep hills, in the Dysynni Valley. Lt Cmdr Charlie Jewitt RN is the only serving Naval Officer I know who regularly hunts hounds. The steepness of the hills is shown with the Master following his pack, as they draw upwards, for a hare.

Once they found, those little beagles ran well, with a splendid cry, which really echoed, as they raced through an ancient, Welsh oak wood, on the side of one of those steep hills.

Stone Valley Hunt, New York, USA

With a colourful backdrop of tree clad hills, English Huntsman John Tulloch walking his pack of Penn-Marydel Hounds on exercise from their kennels at Windswept Farm. Bringing up the rear is Irish Whipper-in Ivan Dowling.

With hounds at the end of an excellent early season hunt, on 22 September 2001 are (L to R) Joseph Forman MFH, Ivan Dowling Whipper-in, John Tulloch Huntsman, Carol Philhower Whipper-in, Susan Orsini MFH.

145

Teme Valley Hunt
With marvellous open country of the Welsh Marches on all sides, Sophie Blain, Master since 1993, leads the way on a cold and windy day.

Hounds hunting slowly along an old sheep path, close to the 1,800 foot summit of 'The Beacon' in Radnorshire, with miles of spectacular, open country behind.

Timber
Going well together during a hunt with the Ludlow are Brian Perry and young rider Fay Hopkins.

Chris Snowball, who was a Joint Master of the Bedale Hunt 1992-2000, jumping timber alongside the River Swale, following a meet at Maunby, North Yorkshire.

Jumping upsides each other, during a hunt with the Pytchley, are Vanessa Barrow and Serena McCall.

The longest serving professional huntsman with a pack of foxhounds in the UK, is Sidney Bailey, who has carried the horn with the Vale of White Horse Hunt, since 1966.

Brigadier Barney White-Spunner who commanded the British led mission to Macedonia, previously commanded The Household Cavalry and was also in charge of the 16 Air Assault Brigade. In between times he edits Baily's Hunting Directory *and writes about hunting in* The Field *magazine.*

Jumping a trappy place in pouring rain is Sarah Voller, Joint Master of the Avon Vale Hunt.

149

Popular Joint Master of the Cottesmore Hunt in High Leicestershire, Charlie Gordon-Watson in action. His sister Mary is a past World Champion Three Day Event rider.

Long serving Joint Master of The Duke of Buccleuch's Hunt, in Scotland, Joe Scott Plummer, among typical grass country.

Toronto and North York Hunt, Canada

With a huge mounted field disappearing over the hill, huntsman Mark Powell leads hounds to draw, past fields of uncut corn. This is very close to their marvellous new kennel complex, opened in August 2002.

With the colourful foliage of Coon Covert in the background, Welsh Huntsman Mark Powell takes his good looking pack of modern English foxhounds to draw another wood. Their bitch 'Havoc', was Grand Champion at the Virginia Hound Show 1999.

Unique

As far as I know, certainly during the past fifty years, there has only been one person to have been Master and Huntsman of a pack of foxhounds in America and then, held the same post in England. This man is Tommy Wright, who was Master and Huntsman of the Triangle Hunt in North Carolina from 1964–79, and whom I enjoyed a day with, after meeting at the home of his Joint Master, Dr J Lee Sedwitz.

In 1980 Tommy Wright came to England, taking the Mastership of the Oakley Hunt, which was founded in 1800. During his two years in office, I spent several days with the Oakley, in what is mostly a plough country, having tea afterwards at their well appointed kennels.

Vale of White Horse Hunt

Sidney Bailey, the longest serving professional huntsman in the country leading hounds to draw past an attractive lake at Linley Hall. Sidney has carried the horn with the VWH since 1966; prior to which he hunted the VWH (Cricklade) from 1961–64 and the now disbanded Wylye Valley 1964–66.

Pictured here during a visit to the hills and woods of the United Pack's country, Sidney Bailey has his good looking hounds busy drawing through frost browned bracken, in search of a fox.

Walls

Randy Waterman, who was a most successful Joint Master and Huntsman of the Piedmont Hounds from 1987–2001, showing good style over a stone wall. He was also a top point to point rider, as are his daughters.

To avoid damaging this wall, the North Staffordshire Hunt have built in a reinforced jumping place; being put to good use by Joint Master Ann Hartley.

A Joint Master of the Vale of White Horse Hunt from 1991–2001, Norman Thomas gives a Gloucestershire stone wall, lots of air.

A stone wall in New York State, being jumped by Susan Orsini, Joint Master of the Stone Valley Hunt.

Judith Goddard makes it look simple as she jumps a Staffordshire Moorland wall, while leading another horse.

Jumping a stone wall in North Yorkshire is Michael Bannister who has been a Joint Master of the Pendle Forest and Craven Hunt since 1977.

Santa Ynez Valley Hunt's Senior Master Steve Lyons, jumping a smart stone wall during a hunt on his 'Kick on Ranch', in California.

The smartly turned out Malcolm Rosser who was Field Master for the Banwen Miners Hunt, flying a stone wall in the hills of South Wales on perfect old turf.

157

Unusual in that he has served the High Peak Harriers as a Joint Master, as Huntsman and latterly as Whipper-in, Martin Brocklehurst must know the country like the back of his hand.

Landing steeply over a Kilkenny wall, Ned Fitzpatrick sat tight, and carried on with barely a pause.

Ware Wires

'The Alternative'?

Warwickshire Hunt

Former Joint Master Jenny Hayward, leading the field on a perfect English autumn morning. She also provided a 'Hunt Breakfast', in honour of the American guests.

Two days after taking part in the Liberty and Livelihood March in London, four of our American foxhunting friends were able to enjoy a beautiful September morning's cub-hunting. Seen here at the end of the day with hounds and Joint Master and Huntsman John Pritchard are (L to R) Warner Ray and Tish Ray, Midland Hunt, Lt. Col. Dennis Foster – Executive Director MFHA, Laura Sloan, Blue Ridge Hunt.

Water

Water is one of hunting's great imponderables; there is either too much, or too little and both have a big effect on sport.

Fording a flooded creek is Leslie Rhett Crosby MFH, Mooreland Hunt, whose father Harry Moore Rhett, founded the Hunt in 1961.

The Mooreland and Live Oak Hounds in full cry after a black coyote in Florida. There is ample evidence of four inches of rain, which had fallen overnight.

Patricia Brennan, Joint Master of the Kilmoganny Hunt, making her way along a flooded Irish lane, with banks of flowering gorse.

Followers of the Vale of White Horse Hunt struggling in flood water, with hounds and hunt staff passing in the background.

The Tanatside Hounds, led by Major Edward Bonnor-Maurice, Joint Master and Huntsman 1971–2001, crossing a swollen stream, during a day's hunting on the Welsh Marches.

The Welsh March to Cardiff

This was organised as a protest against the possible ban on foxhunting in Wales, and went from Machynlleth, to the Welsh Assembly, in Cardiff. Leading the way out of Machynlleth and carrying their banner, are supporters of the Union of Country Sports Workers, of which I am one of the earliest members.

The march leaders, who set a fast pace, head a long line of real hunting supporters, through wonderful Welsh countryside. They cannot imagine life without fox-hunting.

West Hills Hunt, California, USA

This meet, in a grassy canyon at Moor Park is only some twenty miles north west of Los Angeles. The country in places reminded me of the Cattistock hill country in Dorset, except for the working oil wells, dotted here and there!

Here is one of the 'nodding donkey' oil wells, with hounds and Huntsman David Wendler MFH, moving along the floor of a canyon, on their way to draw.

When I took this picture on 11 January 2003 Joint Master and Huntsman David Wendler, was mid way through his fiftieth season carrying the horn with this pack. Initially he served as a professional, before joining the Mastership later on, truly an amazing record for an amazing and popular man.

The mounted followers on the move, only twenty miles north west of Los Angeles, being led by Field Master Harold Ravins, across a huge open landscape in California.

Why Worry Hunt, South Carolina, USA

One of the newest packs in America, having been registered in 1999, with George and Jeanie Thomas as Joint Masters. This photograph well illustrates just how dry their country was in November 2001, with George Thomas and hounds raising the dust, while drawing through a covert.

Joint Master and Huntsman George Thomas, blowing for hounds, in dense undergrowth at the end of a day's hunting, close to their kennels at Windsor. Later we enjoyed a fantastic hunt breakfast, comprising smoked oysters and champagne outdoors and with the temperature showing 75°F!

167

The Worcestershire Hunt

Leading hounds away from Mary Mitchell's Seventieth Birthday Meet, are Huntsman Ian Starsmore and Joint Master Wendy Evans, who was previously a Master of the North Warwickshire Hunt, until they were disbanded, in 1985.

Heavy rain, over an extended period, had left the ground soaked and muddy, as shown by Huntsman Ian Starsmore and his good looking pack of modern English foxhounds.

X-Country Vehicles

Following the Live Oak Hounds in Florida in considerable comfort and elegance are Ken Linthacum, a professional pilot, his wife Diane and, in top hat, Pat Schuh. All are properly turned out, in The Live Oak Hunt uniform.

Out with The Ludlow Hunt on a cold and muddy day, are Kennel-Huntsman Dave Finlay and Lynne Williams. With them, and well wrapped up against the wind, are Dominic and George Finlay and Rhys Williams, who are all mad about hunting.

Xercising Hounds

It was bitterly cold when I walked out with the David Davies Hounds, and Huntsman David Jones, following overnight snow, at their Llandinam kennels in mid-Wales.

Huntsman Anthony Adams, leading the Heythrop's modern English foxhounds, on exercise from the kennels at Chipping Norton in Oxfordshire, on puppy show day in July.

Bicycles are much in evidence as long serving Huntsman Michael Rowson, heads the South Shropshire Hounds on road exercise, with lovely open country as a background.

What an attractive sight the Limerick Hunt's Old English foxhounds make as Joint Master and Huntsman Hugh Robards leads them along a narrow Irish lane, during the summer.

With their brand new kennel complex spreading out behind, Huntsman Mark Powell and Whipper-in Diane Todhunter, walk out with the Toronto and North York Hounds, on a cold morning in Canada.

The Misty Morning Hounds, passing a palm tree in Florida, led by Joint Master and Huntsman Alexis Macaulay, during morning exercise, near the Gainesville Kennels.

Young Riders
'Look Dad, no hands' says Wendi Wilson, whose father 'Epp' Wilson, is Joint Master and Huntsman of the Belle Meade Hunt in Georgia.

Courtney Hensley in full flight, over an unusual obstacle, during a hunt with the Misty Morning Hounds, in Florida, USA.

Well over a coop in the Edisto-Mount Vintage country in South Carolina, is Junior Whipper-in Stephanie Di Franco.

Freddie Beaumont expertly slips his reins as his muddy grey clears an unusual log jump, during a hunt with the Ludlow.

The Ystrad-Taf Fechan Hunt

Huntsman Alwyn Williams hacking the Taf Fechan Hounds back to kennels at the end of a day from Ystradfellte. During a hunt in this glorious wild Welsh countryside Alwyn had a stirrup leather break, but he carried on to the finish, with the fox being accounted for.

This Hunt was formed in 1996, with the amalgamation of the two packs, whose names are now combined. Glyn Powell, who hunted the Ystrad, is taking his hounds to a fresh draw along a Welsh lane in company with the Master Tom Morgan. Glyn's son Mark Powell has been Huntsman to the Toronto and North York Hounds in Canada since 1996.

Zetland Hunt

Huntsman David Jukes
signals the end of a hunt,
as hounds catch their fox
in a field of oil seed rape
after a chase of forty-five
minutes.

'Home' being blown at
the end of the day, stolen
from the weather when
fog looked likely to cause
a cancellation. With
hounds are Whipper-in
Matthew Tunmore,
Huntsman David Jukes
and Joint Master Paul
Morrison.
'Good Night'!